I0828925

SERMONS

PREACHED BEFORE THE CONGREGATION OF THE

PRESBYTERIAN CHURCH,

CORNER OF FIFTH AVENUE AND NINETEENTH STREET,

AT THE

"MEMORIAL SERVICES"

OCTOBER 9, 1859.

APPOINTED IN REFERENCE TO THE DEATH OF THEIR LATE PASTOR,

JAMES WADDEL ALEXANDER, D.D.

BY

CHARLES HODGE, D.D.,

AND

JOHN HALL, D.D.

PUBLISHED AT THE REQUEST OF THE SESSION OF THE CHURCH

NEW-YORK:
ANSON D. F. RANDOLPH,
683 BROADWAY.

1859.

SERMON

BY

CHARLES HODGE, D.D.

SERMON.

"He preached Christ."—Acts 9 : 20.

Nothing higher than this can be said of any man. Angels stand uncovered round the humblest tomb on which these words are inscribed. And so do we. The feeling which has gathered this audience; which now fills every breast, bows every head, and moistens every eye, is reverential love for him who in this desk preached Christ. Had he discoursed on any other theme, though with the tongue of angels, and although he possessed all knowledge, so as to unfold all mysteries, he had been admired and forgotten. Associated as he is with your knowledge of Christ, your experience of his grace, your hope of salvation, you at least never can forget him.

1. In preaching Christ, he preached that Jesus of Nazareth is the true Messiah. As Paul was

pressed in spirit, and testified that Jesus was Christ, and as Apollos mightily convinced the Jews, and that publicly, showing by the Scriptures that Jesus was Christ; so, from this desk, you have been taught that all the promises and predictions relating to the person and work of the Messiah refer to Jesus of Nazareth. You have been taught that he is the seed of the woman who was to bruise the serpent's head; the seed of Abraham in whom all the nations of the earth are to be blessed; the Son of David who was to sit as king on Zion; whose dominion is to stretch from the river to the ends of the earth; who was to be a light to the Gentiles and the glory of his people Israel; who was to bear the sins of many, and make intercession for transgressors; before whom the kings of the earth were to shut their mouths, and to whom every knee shall bow, and every tongue confess that he is Lord.

2. He preached that this Jesus is the Son of God. So Paul preached Christ in the synagogues, that He is the Son of God. Here Christ has been constantly held up as the second person of the Godhead, the eternal Word, who created all things, visible and invisible, and who upholdeth all things by the word of his power. For this incarnate God, your profoundest adoration

has been demanded, your supreme love, the obedience of the conscience, and the devotion of the life. He has been presented as the proper object of the religious affections; and you have been called upon to receive him as God in your inner life, and taught that spiritual and eternal life consists in fellowship with the Son of God, in knowing, worshipping, and serving him. You have been warned that to deny the Son is to deny God altogether; that to profess to worship God, and yet not to worship the Son, is a contradiction; that if to any the glory of God in Christ be hid, they are lost; that there is no clearer manifestation of God; that if men do not believe in light as luminous, they can not believe in light as a fluid diffused through space; if they do not believe in fire, they can not believe in heat as latent; if they do not believe in God as seen, they can not believe in God as unseen. Christ has therefore been here preached as the true God and eternal life.

3. When beset with all manner of doubts; when all around you seemed dark, and no certainty as to truth was from any source to be obtained, Christ has been presented to you as the faithful and true witness. He has been exhibited as the Word, the Revealer, the source of all certain knowledge. You have not been taught to

regard truth as something to be attained by research or received on the testimony of reason. Reason here sits veiled at the feet of Jesus, and hears from his lips the answer to her anxious question: What is truth? His answer carries with it its own evidence. Luminous and illuminating, it enlightens the understanding, it harmonizes with our consciousness, so that every chord vibrates in unison with his celestial voice. As the heavens are high above the earth, and can not be disturbed by the power of man, so faith founded on the teaching of Christ, is exalted above all the assaults of skepticism. In this sense you have been taught that Christ is of God made unto us wisdom.

4. When burdened with a sense of guilt, and disturbed by a fearful looking for judgment, a judgment all the more fearful because felt to be deserved, and apprehended as inevitable; in this pulpit Christ has been preached as your righteousness. You have been taught to regard your own works, all you can either do or suffer, as utterly unavailing. You have been pointed to the Son of God, clothed in our nature, made under the law, fulfilling all its demands, working out for you in your name and in your behalf, a righteousness which satisfies all the requirements of justice, and whose merit is commensurate with the infinite

dignity of Him whose righteousness it is. Clothed in this spotless robe, you feel secure even before the bar of God. The man by whose instrumentality you have been thus clothed with the righteousness of God, and made partakers of that peace which passes all understanding, must have appeared to you as Paul appeared to the Galatians; as an angel from heaven, as one sent of God, to deliver you from everlasting perdition, and to place your feet upon a rock against which neither your own sins nor the gates of hell ever can prevail. As Moses lifted up the serpent in the wilderness, so has Christ been here lifted up, and you have looked on him, and live.

5. Your lamented pastor ever preached Christ as your sanctification. When oppressed with the consciousness of pollution and helplessness; when convinced that you could not change your own hearts, could not repent, could not even feel your guilt or mourn over your corruptions; when your heart as been as a stone, and your constant lamentation was, that you could not make yourself holy, or in any measure prepare yourself to receive the grace of God, he endeavored to convince you that you were acting like a deformed child, who should try to make itself beautiful before it could trust its mother's love. He unfolded to you the mys-

tery of sanctification, by showing you that it is the love of Christ produces holiness, and not holiness in us that produces the love of Christ; that he loves us, not because we are lovely, but makes us lovely by the assurance of his love. He led you to see that your life is hid with God in Christ, that it is not you that live, but Christ that liveth in you; and therefore that the only possible way in which you can ever be delivered from the dominion of sin, and transformed into the image of God, is not by any efforts of your own, not by any educational process, not by acts of self-denial or penance, not by the efficacy of any external rites, but by believing that Christ loves you, notwithstanding your unworthiness, and by receiving from him the gift of the Holy Ghost. In other words, Christ has here been presented as the only source of sanctification, as his righteousness is the only ground of justification.

6. He who so long filled this pulpit, preached Christ as a Redeemer, not only in the sense already mentioned, as freeing us from the condemnation and power of sin, but as the deliverer from all evil. He has been here exhibited as clothed with almighty power, imbued with infinite wisdom and love, pledged to save his people from the allurements of the world, from the machinations of Satan, and from the power of their enemies; as

raising them above the cares and sorrows of this life, sustaining them in times of trial and in the hour of death, and delivering them at last even from the power of the grave, and presenting them faultless in soul and body, before the throne of God, as the trophies of his redeeming grace.

You will bear me witness that he whose departure we so much lament, did preach Christ as the Messiah, as the eternal Son of God, as the only source of truth, as our righteousness, sanctification, and redemption. From Sabbath to Sabbath, publicly, and from house to house, he testified that this is the true grace of God; and thus preaching, he was made of God to you a savor of life unto life.

But how was he so eminently fitted thus to preach? His first and most important, and, indeed, indispensable qualification for this work, was, that he himself knew Christ. He had not only that knowledge which is attained by the study of the Scriptures, and learning what is therein revealed concerning the person and work of Christ, but that knowledge which is due to the inward revelation by the Spirit. Paul says that it pleased God to reveal his Son in him, that he might preach him among the Gentiles. He does not refer here to the outward manifestation of Christ which arrested him on his way to Damascus, but to an inward revelation therewith connected. It was a spiritual illumination by which he was enabled to see the glory of God in the face of Jesus Christ. One glimpse of that glory transformed the blaspheming persecutor into the humble, adoring, devoted servant of the Lord Jesus. It was such a revelation that made your pastor what he was. Without this, all his other gifts had been of no account.

It is, however, an instructive fact, that the apostle who labored, suffered, and accomplished more than all the others, was the one most richly endowed with natural abilities and acquired knowledge. When these gifts are relied upon, and especially when they are made the ground of self-glorification, they are like the fire of thorns, brilliant and noisy, but which soon goes out in darkness, leaving nothing but ashes to be scattered by the wind. But when their possessor feels as Paul felt, that he is nothing, and can do nothing; when he relies, not on his powers of persuasion, but solely upon the demonstration of the Spirit, then God condescends to use them for his own glory and for the edification of the Church.

The Rev. James W. Alexander was therefore what he was as a preacher of Christ, not only because he was a devout worshipper of Christ, but also because he was endowed with varied natural gifts, improved by a long process of culture and discipline.

He was born March 13th, 1804, in Louisa County, Virginia, in the house of his maternal grandfather, the Rev. Dr. Waddel, of blessed memory, by whom he was consecrated to God in baptism. His father was the late Archibald Alexander, D.D., the representative man of the Church for our age and country, to whom he was largely indebted for his religious, literary, and theological training. After enjoying the instructions of the most eminently classical teacher of his day, for some years, in Philadelphia, he completed his academical career in the College of New-Jersey, in the year 1820. He was appointed a tutor in that venerable institution while he was pursuing his studies in the Theological Seminary at Princeton. In 1825 he was licensed to preach the Gospel. The following year he became the pastor of the church at Charlotte Court House, Virginia—a church which his venerated father had previously served, and to which his own son has recently been called. He was forced to relinquish that charge on account of the failure of his health, and in 1829 he settled in Trenton, N. J., as pastor of the First Presbyterian Church in that city. In 1833 he was elected Professor of Belles Lettres in the College at Princeton. He discharged the duties of that office with eminent success for eleven years. In 1844 he became the pastor of the Duane street Church, New-York, whence he was called by the General Assembly of our Church to fill the chair of Ecclesiastical History and Church Government in the Theological Seminary at Princeton. A few years' experience convinced him that the sedentary duties of a professor were not suited to his peculiar constitution, and therefore in 1851 he accepted the charge of this church, in the service of which he remained until God called him to a higher service in heaven.

This recital is sufficient to show how varied and abundant were his means of culture and experience. He never filled a post which he did not adorn, and never left a charge that the people did not mourn over his departure as a sad bereavement. He has died in the rich maturity of his years and usefulness, leaving behind him no superior, and few if any equals in the sphere in which he acted. The labors and cares of the pastoral office over such a church, and in such a city as this, had so worn on his sensitive frame, that early in the last spring he was obliged to intermit his services, and seek the renewal of his strength among the mountains of his native State.

Every thing promised speedy and complete recovery. You were looking forward with confidence to his return to his home and pulpit, when the sad intelligence reached you, that God had otherwise ordained. A few days' illness from an acute disease disappointed all your hopes. Early on the morning of the last Sabbath of July, just as the first rays of the sun gilded the tops of the surrounding mountains, the glories of heaven broke on his enraptured gaze.

Dr. Alexander united in himself gifts and graces rarely found in combination. God had endowed him with a retentive memory and a perspicacious intellect, with great power of application and acquirement, with singular delicacy of taste, with a musical ear, and a resonant voice. These gifts were all cultivated and turned to the best account. Probably no minister in our Church was a more accomplished scholar. He was familiar with English literature in all periods of its history. He cultivated the Greek and Latin, French, German, Italian, and Spanish languages, not merely as a philologist, but for the treasures of knowledge and of taste which they contain. To this wide compass of his studies is in good measure to be referred many of his characteristics as a writer, the abundance of his literary allusions, his curious felicity of expression, and the variety of his imagery. Many of his productions are like strings of pearls; each sentence complete in its own beauty, and all connected by an invisible thread. His facility of production was wonderful. He would often accomplish in days what few men could accomplish in as many weeks. He used his pen as if it were a living member of his body, and found a positive pleasure in its exercise. He was a frequent contributor to literary and religious journals. The *Princeton Review* is indebted to him for many of its most valuable contributions, not a few of which have been reprinted both in this country and in England. More than thirty volumes on the Catalogue of the American Sunday-School Union are from his pen. To these are to be added his more elaborate works, long familiar to the Christian public in Great Britain and America.

It was, however, not only in the department of literature that Dr. Alexander was thus distinguished. He was an erudite theologian. Few men were more conversant with the writings of the early fathers, or more familiar with Christian doctrine in all its phases. He embraced the faith of the Reformed Churches in its integrity with a strength of conviction which nothing but the accordance of that system with his religious experience could produce. A faith founded on argument may be shaken by argument; but a conviction of truth arising from religious experience, that is, from a state of consciousness produced by the Spirit of God, is not to be moved. Theology and philosophy are so related, that devotion to the former involves of necessity the cultivation of the latter. Dr. Alexander was therefore at home in the whole department of philosophical speculation. His last publication was an able exposition of the views of the metaphysicians of the middle ages on one of the most important questions in mental science.

Thus richly and variously was your beloved pastor endowed. These gifts, however, were but accomplishments. Underneath these adornments, in themselves of priceless value, was the man and the Christian. He was an Israelite without guile. Probably no man living was freer from all envy and jealousy, from, malice, hypocrisy, and evil-speaking. No one ever heard of his saying or doing an unseemly or unkind thing. The associations connected with his name in the minds of all who knew him, are of things true, just, pure, lovely, and of good report. No one can think of him without being the happier and the better for the thought. He was a delightful companion. His varied knowledge, his humor, his singular power of illustration rendered his conversation, when in health and spirits, a perpetual feast. Having been brought early in life to a saving knowledge of the truth, his religious knowledge and experience were profound and extensive. He was therefore a skillful casuist, a wise counsellor, and abundantly able to comfort the afflicted with the consolation wherewith he himself had been comforted of God. He was eminently a devout man, reverential in all his acts and utterances, full of faith and of the Holy Ghost.

The pulpit was his appropriate sphere. There all his gifts and graces, all his acquirements and experiences found full scope. Hence the remarkable variety which characterized his preaching; which was sometimes doctrinal, sometimes experimental, sometimes historical, sometimes descriptive or graphic, bringing scriptural scenes and incidents as things present before the mind; often exegetical, unfolding the meaning of the word of God in its own divine form. Hence, too, the vivacity of thought, the felicity of style, and fertility of illustration which were displayed in all his sermons. He could adapt himself to any kind of audience. When a Professor in the College, he acted as a voluntary pastor of an African church in Princeton, and we have heard him say that he regarded the sermons which he preached to that congregation the best he ever delivered. As we remarked in the commencement of this discourse, he preached Christ in a manner which seemed to many altogether peculiar. He endeavored to turn the minds of men away from themselves, and to lead them to look only unto Jesus. He strove to convince his hearers that the work of salvation had been accomplished for them, and was not to be done by them; that their duty was simply to acquiesce in the work of Christ, assured that the subjective work of sanctification is due to the objective work of Christ, as appropriated by faith and applied by the Holy Ghost. He thus endeavored to cut off the delays, the anxieties, and misgivings which arise from watching the exercises of our own minds, seeking in what we inwardly experience a warrant for accepting what is outwardly offered to the chief of sinners, without money and without price. He was eminently successful in his ministry, not only in the conversion of sinners, but in comforting and edifying believers. The great charm of his preaching, that to which more than to any thing else its efficiency is to be referred, was his power over the religious affections. He not only instructed, encouraged, and strengthened his hearers, but he had, to a remarkable degree, the gift of calling their devotional feelings into exercise. In his prayers there were those peculiar intonations to which the Spirit of God alone can attune the human voice, and at the sound of which the gates of heaven seem to unfold, and the worshippers above and the worshippers on earth mingle together, prostrate in adoration. Your religious services, under his ministry, were truly seasons of devotion, the highest form of enjoyment vouchsafed to men on earth. The man who can give us this enjoyment, who can thus raise our hearts to God, and bring us into communion with our Saviour, we reverence and love. This is a power which no one envies, from which no one wishes to detract, which surrounds its possessor with a sacred halo, attracting all eyes and offending none.

Dr. Alexander's preëminence, therefore, was due not to any one gift alone; not to his natural abilities, to his varied scholarship, to his extensive theological knowledge and religious experience; not to his divine unction, or to his graces of elocution. It was the combination of all these which made him, not the first of orators to hear on rare occasions, but the first of preachers to sit under, month after month and year after year.

Dr. Alexander was a man of sorrows. Frequent family bereavements, repeated attacks of illness, some of them attended by great bodily agony, a shattered nervous constitution, caused him a degree of suffering protracted through many years, known fully only to God and to his own heart. As he entered heaven, a voice might be heard saying: "This is one who has come out of great tribulation, and has washed his robes and made them white in the blood of the Lamb."

The death of such a man is an irreparable loss. God indeed will raise up other instruments to carry on his work, but no one can ever supply his place to his immediate relatives, to his life-long friends, and to his children in the faith. They all must carry with them to the grave a wound which knows no healing. Such sorrow, however, is not like the sorrow of the world, which worketh death. It is the tribute which we willingly pay to those we love. It is not inconsistent with joy and gratitude in the remembrance of all that he was to us and to the Church. He was one of the blessed of the Lord. Blessed in his parentage, in his early conversion, in his abundant gifts, in his long-continued and eminent usefulness, in the admiration, love, and confidence of the people of God. He has finished his course, he kept the faith, and henceforth there is laid up for him a crown of righteousness which the Lord the righteous Judge will give him at that day.

In view of such a life and such a destiny, earthly distinctions sink into nothing. No man is so hardened, that he would not a thousand times prefer to be what your beloved pastor was and is, than to possess all of wealth and power the world has to give.

As this discourse began with the name of Christ, so let it end. The worship of Christ is our religion; the service of Christ our loyal duty; and the enjoyment of Christ is our heaven. The sum and substance of the preaching ever heard within these walls, is, that Christ is the only source of truth, of righteousness, of holiness, and of eternal life, so that we are complete in him. To Him, therefore, be honor and glory, might, majesty, and dominion, world without end. Amen.

SERMON

BY

JOHN HALL, D.D.

SERMON.

"Moreover, I will endeavor that ye may be able, after my decease, to have these things always in remembrance."—2 Peter 1 : 15.

The decease of a minister of the Gospel—of one who, as well as the writer of this sentence, may be called "a servant and an apostle of Jesus Christ"—is an event of the most solemn interest.

It is such to the minister himself, whilst yet contemplated by him in anticipation: for he knows that, besides his own personal standing at the final judgment, he is bound to watch for the souls of others as one that must give account—and this with joy or grief, according, not only as he will have to testify respecting those to whom he has ministered the Gospel, but as he himself has been faithful to his trust. It is at his decease he is to discover whether he has both saved himself and them that heard him; whether he shall receive from the Chief Shepherd a crown of glory that fadeth not away, or having preached to others be himself a castaway.

His own decease is also a solemn contemplation to a minister, because he knows that his work is to survive him. His preaching, his example, his whole influence, are not as transitory as his own brief life. Neither the good nor the evil of his course will be buried with him. His faithfulness or his negligence will primarily affect those whom he immediately served, but the consequences may descend through that generation to those who will inherit the opinions and the spirit of their fathers. He may leave behind him such permanent records of his life and of his sentiments, that successive ages will reap the benefit or the injury, as effectually as if they had heard his voice, or been familiar with his company. It was the ambition—the "endeavor"—of Paul, so long as he was "in this tabernacle," so to present the glorious doctrines and precepts of the Gospel, what he in the text, for the fifth time in the chapter, emphatically calls "these things," that believers, consistently with their obligations and his own, might be able after his decease to have them always in remembrance.

Thus the decease of a minister is an event of

great moment also to the Church; and this in proportion as he reached them by his preaching, his intercourse, his writings, his reputation, his personal character. In all these respects none stand so close to a minister as the people whom he has most directly served as a pastor and a teacher. They knew him best. They loved him most. They can most justly appreciate him. They saw him; they heard him; they read him. They remember the tones of his voice, the expression of his countenance. They have local, sacred associations with his person; he is recalled to them as he stood in the pulpit, as he poured forth his soul in prayer, as he united with them in the songs of worship, as he broke to them with tremulous emotion, the bread of the Lord's table, as he stretched his hands over them in benediction, as he committed their children to God's covenant in baptism, as he came to them when they were in trouble, consoled them in bereavement, soothed them in sickness, brought them both temporal and spiritual relief in necessity, was to them, in all circumstances, not merely an official or professional attendant, but a sympathizing friend; and above all, or rather in connection with all else, they remember how in private intercourse, as well as in his public ministrations, he sought with the tenderness of a brother and the faithfulness of a messenger of Christ Jesus, to awaken, or admonish, or comfort, or instruct, or encourage, or guide; by any means, and according to the demands of each case, to bring the soul to the Saviour, to the word of his grace, to the converting and sanctifying Spirit, to the full joy and peace of believing.

Ah! my brethren, have I touched your hearts as this outline has brought before you the image of your own pastor?—our own beloved Alexander? And do I indeed stand here to-day to speak of *his* "decease"?—to call to your "remembrance" the things he has said, instead of hearing them again from his own lips, as you fondly hoped to do this very day, when, in a manner he so gratefully appreciated, you prevailed upon him to suspend his labors that he might recover strength! What a different occasion this from that which you anticipated! How little you thought when you closed your sanctuary a few weeks ago, that when you should enter it again, that new tablet would meet your eyes! But the event was not as surprising to him as to you. I believe that when he set out on his journey he was disposed, without any morbid presentiment, to say: "And now behold I know that ye all, among whom I have gone preaching the kingdom of God, shall see my face no more."

But in the midst of these personal sorrows, let us not overlook either the comforts or the obligations that remain. Let us listen again to the instructions of the text, that the influence of a faithful minister goes beyond his decease, and that, on the part of his people, both the benefits and responsibilities of their sundered relation continue. If ever a servant and apostle of Jesus Christ labored less for momentary effect and personal ends, and mere lifetime results, than to lay such foundations as would cause the saving truth to be had in remembrance after his departure, it was he whose voice has scarcely ceased to echo in this house. The instructions he imparted were so weighty as to be worth remembrance, and so well conveyed as to defy all but wilful forgetfulness. His decease has not arrested his sermons, his visits, his counsels, his character. Being dead, he yet speaketh; every thing recalls him; and your minds, my brethren, will be treacherous to the tenderest and weightiest impressions that are ever directed to them, if they do not remember both him and his words. He did not seek your applause; he did not labor for fame; he did not graduate his love and care for you by his own brief years; he did not measure the extent of his responsibility by the ephemeral judgment of his fellow-creatures: it was the permanent, eternal result as to himself and you, that he kept before him. And so, if he could speak to us to-day, he would not ask us for our eulogies; he would not be intent on learning the amount of our admiration, but he would plead with us again to have always in remembrance "these things" which concern life and salvation; or as Paul elsewhere says, "By which ye are saved, if ye keep in memory what I preached unto you," (1 Cor. 15;) or as the Divine Master himself said, after his resurrection, to his disciples: "These are the words which I spake unto you while I was yet with you . . . and ye are witnesses of these things." (Luke 24.)

Whatever helped to make a minister efficient whilst living, will contribute to enforce and prolong his influence after his decease. The remembrance of the truth he ministered will be assisted by the remembrance of all that qualified him for his usefulness and characterized it; by all that marked him as designed and authorized to be an ambassador of Christ. We may hope, therefore, to aid the practical and permanent objects before us this day and not depart from their legitimate connection with the Lord's day and the Lord's house, by adverting to some of those particulars in which we may discern the arrangements of Providence to qualify our deceased brother for the work assigned him, and which were completed and crowned in his ministry with this congregation.

The beginnings of these Providential designs are to be traced to his pious ancestry, and above all, to his immediate parentage. Inheriting the Christian birthright through both lines of descent, grandson of the country pastor whose name he bore, and whose venerable person is an historical portrait in our literature*—it is as the son of Archibald and Janetta Alexander, that we of this day are assured that it was his lot not only to be baptized in the name, but trained in the nurture and admonition of the Lord Jesus. It was while his eminent father was yet President of Hampden Sidney College, that this son was born, (March 13, 1804,) at the house of his grandfather, Waddel, in Louisa; but he was only in his fourth year when the residence of the family was removed to Philadelphia, (December, 1807,) and he was not nine when (July, 1812,) they removed to Princeton, upon the opening of the Theological Seminary.

The love for his native southern State and for the city of his childhood in the Middle States, left marks on his character which show that these early footsteps of his life had their influence in expanding his patriotic and Christian affections

* Wirt's *British Spy*.

beyond any sectional or local limits; a quality of indispensable consequence to the preparation for a ministry which is to know no man after the flesh, and to be governed by none of the prejudices or fanaticisms so apt to grow out of the associations of one's continued residence in the spot of his nativity, and inexperience in the actual condition of society in other sections.

His education in the College of New-Jersey, in the close association of his family with the Theological school, and the comparatively few students of its first years, is to be regarded among the preliminary steps of the youth in the course of Divine designation. That designation was as yet concealed; for whilst every thing in the literary and religious life around him, in his own dwelling and in the public institutions and men which give fame to the village, was as favorable as outward circumstances could be to the highest intellectual excitement and the earliest religious impressions, it was not until his college course was closing, that he became thoroughly awakened to his great advantages and responsibilities in either respect. But even then, he was only in his seventeenth year. At that period, having been graciously brought to a clear apprehension of his spiritual condition, he made his first public profession of faith. (April, 1821.)

It was while at College that the saving change occurred; and the language of a letter written some time afterward strikingly coincides with the sentiments of his dying-bed, when he says: "There can not certainly be on earth any greater pleasure than to see without doubt one's self condemned justly by God's law, and at the same time saved freely by the sovereign mercy of God in Christ. The satisfaction which I then felt in committing all my cares and concerns, my soul and body into the hands of a Saviour whose infinitely lovely character I then saw, I never expect to receive from any other source." How similar in sentiment is this to the expression of his last hours! "If the curtain were now to drop and I were this moment ushered into the presence of my Maker, I would first prostrate myself in an unutterable sense of my nothingness and guilt; but secondly, I would look up to my Redeemer with an inexpressible assurance of faith and love."

Immediately after his graduation, (August, 1820,) he betook himself to a course of private study of the subject he had slighted in College. He gave two years to this object, and principally to classical reading, before entering the third class of the Theological school, which he did in the autumn of 1822; taking up his abode, like the students from abroad, in the edifice itself. The letters of his years in the Seminary are eloquent with description of his enjoyment of the studies and of the companionship of the band of congenial minds, with whom the topics of the class-room were subjects of animated discussion in their more private and social encounters. Those unrestrained communications also reveal the discipline by which the heart of the future preacher, pastor, and consoler, was learning how to speak to multitudes from the resources of a deep personal experience. Even in that early period of his life, he was becoming acquainted with the violent and sudden alternations to which his delicate temperament continued subject, from the highest pitch of joyous excitement to the depths of melancholy and indescribable misery.

Yes, my brethren, it is a somewhat painful, yet in all respects an impressive and interesting reflection for those who have obtained so much relief, so much sympathy, so much instruction from the tenderness of your late pastor, from the heart-reaching power of his discourses, his conversations, his whole intercourse, to know that to qualify him for this service, the wise and gracious foresight of Almighty God saw it necessary to lead his disciple from his earliest Christian walk, in the path of some of the most poignant and overwhelming distresses that can oppress the human soul. Ascribe it to what immediate cause we may, to delicate or disordered nerves, to morbid sensibilities, whether physical or moral, to excessive intellectual excitement, to preternatural susceptibility to the extremes of enjoyment and suffering, we know from the result, that this part of experience familiar to him in a greater or less measure from his youth to his last days, was the means sanctified to the production and maintenance of that depth, fullness, and richness of his spiritual traits, which laid the foundation of and gave the predominant characteristics and direction to his piety and his influence. For you—for us all—he thus suffered; through these sufferings he was borne by the same grace which meted them out, so that I do not believe that the Apostle Paul could say with more grateful consciousness than could your pastor: "Blessed be God, even the Father of our Lord Jesus Christ, the Father of mercies, and the God of all comfort; who comforteth us in all our tribulation, that we may be able to comfort them which are in any trouble, by the comfort wherewith we ourselves are comforted of God. For as the sufferings of Christ abound in us, so our consolation also aboundeth by Christ. And whether we be afflicted, it is for your consolation and salvation, which is effectual in the enduring of the same sufferings which we also suffer; or whether we be comforted, it is for your consolation and salvation."

Think of this fact, my brethren, in estimating both what it cost to provide you with such a Pastor as you have had, and what responsibility you are under now—after his decease—to have in your remembrance the rich fruits of such a painful culture. These were among the signs of his calling to the discipleship and apostleship of the cross. He bore in his body the marks of the Lord Jesus. (Gal. 6.) But he could continue, till the close of his suffering life, to adopt, as he did thirty-five years ago, the expressions of Madame Guion's hymn, in Cowper's translation, when, personifying Sorrow, it says:

"It costs me no regret that she
Who followed Christ should follow me:
And though where'er she goes,
Thorns spring spontaneous at her feet,
I love her—and extract a sweet
From all my bitter woes."

And with equal sincerity he appropriated these other lines from the same hands:

"Long plunged in sorrow, I resign
My soul to that dear hand of thine,
Without reserve or fear;
That hand shall wipe my streaming eyes,
Or into smiles of glad surprise,
Transform the falling tear.

"My soul's possession is thy love;
In earth beneath, or heaven above
I have no other store:
And though with fervent suit I pray,
And importune thee night and day,
I ask thee nothing more."

After about two years' industrious application in the Seminary he took advantage of an unexpected opening for the improvement of himself simultaneously in learning and teaching, by his appointment as tutor in the College, first of mathematics, then of the languages, (1824.) This position involved him in many petty troubles annoying to one of his temperament, but as he wrote at the time: "I need to be buffeted about a little, to call forth what little energy and firmness I may possess." Here is another item, not too insignificant to be regarded in the work of his preparation for the life of a pastor; that of counteracting his natural tendency to shrink from every thing like authority or discipline over others. So earnestly did he apply himself to meet the demands of his office, that he gave six and a half hours daily to his own private studies besides what was required in the recitation-room. These pursuits were not lost upon the discipline of a mind preparing, as the event has proved, for the logical, clear, precise statements and arguments of gospel preaching, and its defence by the pen, in a style so truly classical.

It was just at this period, too, that his personal Christian experience passed through such a taste, as he said, of the terrors of the Lord, that it seemed to him, at the time, as if he had known nothing before of true conversion. But now he writes, (July 10, 1824:) "I have finally been humbled by the prostration of my own will, which has been since birth, free only to evil, to the point of entire submission to God. . . . God has in mercy brought me to a view of my utter impotence, of the justice of the law which would condemn me to eternal wrath, and of my being helpless in the hands of an Almighty avenger. Henceforth my single aim is to submit myself to God as an instrument in his hands to be used for what he chooses. Death would be a release, should it come this instant; and except to do God's work, I desire not to breathe another moment."

The occupations of the tutorship did not interrupt his theological reading, nor prevent his giving time to the acquisition of several modern languages, natural science and general literature. He had also begun to employ his pen in contributions to a variety of periodical works, religious and literary. Thus his skill in writing and his literary accomplishments were providing for the grace, polish and refinement which were to do so much to commend the highest truth to masses of hearers and readers. It is curious for us in this connection to find him say in a letter of December, 1824: "I tried my abilities at preaching the other night at the Preaching Society of the Seminary. It was the first regular sermon I ever wrote." Perhaps it will not seem less curious to hear him say some months later: "Nothing to which I put my hand ever dissatisfied me so much as sermon-writing. I am enough chagrined after every effort of this kind to throw the thing in the fire. Whatever complacency I may feel in any thing else, my sermons are truly mortifying to me."

The next step in his preparation for the service to which the divine purpose was guiding him, was his obtaining the practice and experience of a pastor, in the comparatively small and secluded bounds of a country congregation. Having been licensed by the Presbytery of New-Brunswick, (October 4, 1825,) he spent some months in Maryland and Virginia, and declining a call to be colleague of the late Dr. Glendy, in Baltimore, he was ordained by the Presbytery of Hanover, and installed over the church in Charlotte Court House. (March 3, 1827.)

Short as was the term of this engagement, the young minister learned valuable lessons in active parochial life, and in the practice of preaching sermons which there was not time to write. Here, too, he underwent the salutary discipline of a serious illness, which compelled him to return to the North, and finally to resign his charge. This made an interruption of a year in his capacity for active labor. But the time was not lost. His faith had a stern probation, and it came all the stronger prepared for future trials, for a more solemn, earnest treatment of the work of life, and for a more sympathetic intercourse with the afflicted. "Death" (this was his testimony at the time) "has been viewed by me as a precious entrance into eternal bliss."

When he resumed his public services, (January, 1829,) it was as pastor of what was then the only Presbyterian congregation in Trenton, New-Jersey. There he continued four years—years, like all the others of his Christian life, marked by the most industrious and varied occupations, by a zealous and successful ministry, by progressive spiritual experience, and in his domestic life by the blending of great joys with great afflictions. During this period, besides his stated employment as a pastor, he had the editorial care of the *Biblical Repertory*, and was the largest contributor to its pages. He was then also employed in that series of writings for the young and for the plans which specially contemplate their benefit, which gave him, for the rest of his life, an intimate connection with the American Sunday-School Union. This predisposition and its cultivation by him, deserve to be remembered among the means of his pastoral efficiency. You know how he loved your children; how he sought to do them good; what anxieties he showed for the youth of this congregation, with all their privileges, and for the youth of this city, with all their exposures and destitutions. You know how he worked and pleaded for the promotion of religious instruction and early piety here, and for the excitement of every patriotic, philanthropic, and religious motive to provide for the universal extension of Christian education. None know better than the children and the young men here, how he loved the souls of youth, yearned for their salvation and trembled for their perils. This object always gave a direction to his labors, caused him to simplify his presentation of truth, and increased the tenderness of his spirit towards his people as families.

It was while in Trenton that he tried to stir up others to do what in subsequent years he himself did so well, when he asks, "Could not a series of 'Letters to Working Men' be put in some popular journal, commending honest labor, asserting the rights of mechanics, but unveiling the deformity of the levelling system?" which he apprehended was about to inflict irreparable damage, moral as well as political, on our country. This was the germ of the thoughts and counsels that are now so attractively realized in the volumes of "The American Mechanic" and "The Working Man." It was while at Trenton that he was for some time employed on a laborious commentary on the Gospels, intended for Sunday-schools, but abandoned on finding that another hand (the Rev. Mr. Barnes) had undertaken a similar work. His pen was never at rest. In prose and poetry, in books, reviews, and fugitive pieces; in translations from the Latin and German; in copious notes on his reading, which was in all departments of knowledge; in sermons and letters, his manuscript work was already portending the vast bulk it attained. With it all he never intermitted the daily study of the Scriptures in both the originals; and as he generally observed a methodical theological course in his morning discourses, he maintained through the week a continuous systematic study of divinity. His theological studies were at all times almost purely exegetical. To discover, by original research, the meaning of the Bible, was his first aim; and human opinions in the shape of bodies of divinity, or commentaries, were only accepted by him as auxiliary to his independent research. The Greek Concordance was his great Commentary. His favorite religious reading was Biography and Experimental Piety. "No works," he observed, "have ever given me healthier impulses in my religious course than those of the English Nonconformists of the seventeenth century." The type, alike of his Theology and Piety, is indicated by this allusion to his choice books. I may further define, once for all, what I believe to have been his position to the last on these points, by referring to Russell's 'Letters Practical and Consolatory,' published in Edinburgh about 1830, and of which he said in 1834: "I have read no human production which comes nearer my views of Calvinism: it is theology without one shred of scholasticism; orthodoxy without one film of mystification; purity without one knot of ecclesiastical harshness." This opinion of a work, so unpretending in its design, is eminently demonstrative of what was your Pastor's estimate of an experimental above a merely technical theology, and of what was the habit of his mind to find the strongest attractions of the Gospel, in its character as at once "practical" and "consolatory." All this, too, with the full erudition and power that when occasion came, showed that if he was not a polemic by practice, it was not for want of the requisite ability.

To return to the narrative of his course in Trenton, (which may also be taken as marking the general course of his pastorates afterwards,) I remark that all his engagements were not at the expense of his more immediate duties as a pastor, is attested by the congregation, who remember his punctual and earnest exercises, whenever his health did not arrest them. We may learn something of his methods and diligence by such a paragraph as this in a letter to a friend in 1831: "My breast is quite sore with the unintermitted exertion of lungs in singing and prayer and talking. . . . For the last six evenings I have attended meetings in different precincts. Last Sunday afternoon I preached to the convicts in the State's prison. I think I never felt more the unspeakable privilege of preaching the unsearchable riches of Christ. Last week I conversed with those who are in the cells. . . . I have made some fruitless attempts to have a Bible-class among the blacks. . . . Since I lived in Virginia I feel a peculiar yearning over these poor creatures, and sometimes feel as if I could joyfully devote myself to laboring among them."

It is twenty-eight years since the social meetings referred to in this passage were held, but within a week I have heard one of the many, who will ever remember him as their father in Christ, say, in the recollection of those occasions: "Oh! how he used to sing! I can now hear his clear, loud voice leading the hymn:

'Hearts of stone, relent! relent!'"

In a letter of a later date than the one I have just quoted, alluding to his having declined an invitation to preach for a vacant congregation in one of the largest cities, he says: "If I am to be a pastor, and nothing but necessity could make me willing to be any thing else, I believe I have more openings to serve Christ here than in any more laborious charge. I have counted up about fifty persons with whom I have had religious conversation, and who are more or less tender. I have an access to them which no other person could have for a long time, and which I should not have to the same number elsewhere." You will recognize in another sentence a peculiarity of your deceased pastor which was as marked in his latest as in his earliest years of pastoral connection. "Some of my most delightful hours have been spent in sick-rooms, by dying-beds, or among poor, unlettered believers, or especially in rejoicing with them that do rejoice for the first time in Christ." Yet, he who had such a heart in his work, who was doing so much in spite of a feeble constitution, and had such testimonies to his efficiency, was aspiring to perform so much more than he could do, and was so impatient to see the awakening of all the souls about him, that he was constantly bewailing his lack of love for souls, the unprofitableness of his ministry, and his insignificance as a Christian workman: shrinking, as it were, into obscurity, from which, *never* his own seeking—*only* a compulsory Providence dislodged him.

By these experiences his soul was attaining to deeper humility, his affections to greater tenderness, his zeal for the kingdom of heaven rising and expanding with his labors. Forget not, my brethren, as we thus follow his path, the main design of our undertaking—to keep you in mind of what is to grow out of all this training for his best days in your service, and to be had in remembrance by your souls, now after his decease, as you will have to answer at the great day.

And the spiritual mind, as is so common in the ways of Providence, was still nurtured by painful trials. It was at this period of his life that he received from the Lord that most precious of his domestic blessings which was so graciously spared to him to the last—his happy marriage—

but it was now also that sorrowful, often agonizing, years were laid to his lot in the sufferings and death of children—an anguish to which no parental heart could be more sensitive than his. "How it is with others," he remarked, "I can not tell; but it seems to me that I need a constant series of inward or outward conflicts to make me value Divine comforts."

To the trials and the training of that day must be added those which a temper so peaceful and charitable as his suffered, not so much from the merits of the polemical controversy which then arose in our Church, and afterwards divided it, as from the spirit with which it was too often waged; so that he was sometimes constrained to exclaim: "The greatest heresy is want of love." "Oh! for a cycle of peace," he exclaimed; "Oh! for a breathing-spell from these unnatural contentions! I feel as if I could join with any who would humbly unite in direct and kind efforts to save sinners and relieve human misery. Can not a poor believer go along in his pilgrimage heavenward, without being always on military duty? At judgment, I heartily believe, that some heresies of heart and temper will be charged as worse than heavy doctrinal errors. To you (he adds to his correspondent) I may say this, because you understand me as holding, not merely that the tenets of our Church are true, but that they are very important. But I see how easy it is to 'hold the truth' in rancor and hate, which is the grand error of depraved human nature." These few lines may be taken as exhibiting the moral position which he occupied throughout the conflict of that day ; and this is sufficient for the light in which we are now viewing him. It is more to my purpose to remark, that if he learned more than ever before of the spiritual evil of prejudice, uncharitableness, bigotry—more of the weakness of good men under the excitement of the best motives—more of the evils of strife and contention—more of the importance of the mind's being well grounded in sound doctrine as to all essential truth, and the heart at the same time moulded to the love and charity of the Gospel, then his own painful exercises during that crisis were parts of his discipline for the defence and exemplification of that meekness and forbearance towards all who love the Lord Jesus Christ in sincerity, which marked his intercourse, in the large field of this city, with evangelical ministers and Christians of every name, and his sympathy with every project which his judgment approved, where co-workers of all such denominations were combined. How truly catholic was his spirit was shown, not in the declamations of the public platform, nor perhaps in making what is called the union principle a point of zeal as always the best system of doing good, so much as in his freedom as an ecclesiastic from prejudice and envy, and more especially in his love of holding fellowship with, and deriving instruction from, the unlimited host of good men and practical and devotional writers of all ages and connections. Wherever there was warmth, earnestness, simplicity—wherever there was the spirit of Christ, there was his heart and hand, and I may emphatically add, his voice; singing with Wesley, or Luther, or Gerhardt, or even from the Breviary, as fervently as with Toplady or Watts; and literally praying "with all prayer and supplication," wherever, in old time or in late, in written form or in the gush of the rudest unpremeditation, he found disciples whom Jesus had taught how to pray.

It was the fruit of this enlarged and comprehensive spirit of Charity that we are called upon to have in remembrance now, after his decease, for our own following, as he in it so followed Christ. You have seen how this spirit won his way among all Christian people, gained their confidence, disarmed sectarian mistrust in hearing or reading him, and thus multiplied the number of those who will ever bless God for such a minister and author. In his practice he gave great weight to the axiom: "The servant of the Lord must not strive, but be gentle unto all men . . . patient: in meekness instructing those that oppose themselves." (2 Tim. 2.) And, therefore, he would say even of those whose religion was most antagonistic to his own: "If, instead of reviling the Catholics, we would surpass them in schools, in personal charities, in persevering missions, and in the preparation of our ministers, I believe we should make more head against them."

Discouraging or refusing applications from other quarters of much more prominence, your Pastor remained in Trenton, until his declining health demanded a suspension of pastoral cares; and after some hesitation between his appointment as a Secretary of his favorite institution, the Sunday-School Union, and the offer of the editorial charge of *The Presbyterian*, in Philadelphia, he chose the latter, (1833.) This post gave him a few months of more direct experience in the general interests of the Church, and of the wide-spread and multifarious observation which a religious journalist must exercise. But he thought that a less vexatious, and more retired department would be better suited to his taste and circumstances; and therefore, in the course of the first year of his occupation as an editor, he consented to take the chair of Rhetoric and Belles Lettres, in his own beloved College.

The eleven years (1833–1844) which were then passed in Princeton, though they were withdrawn from the more direct work of the ministry, and this solely on account of the infirmities of his health, were not absorbed in his literary office, or lost to the higher interests of the Church, or to his prospective position in it. His correspondence, throughout that period, has less of the tone of the mere scholar or professor, than of a minister who, in season and out of season, was seeking to spread divine knowledge and to save souls. Submitting patiently to the Providential suspension of his employment as a Pastor, and doing all that industry could do for the faithful discharge of his duties as an instructor, yet one who did not know his professional position, would conclude from his letters, that he was in the centre of weighty and immediate responsibilities for multitudes. His mind labored with schemes for the diffusion of healthful and conservative influences throughout all classes of society. The threatenings of infidelity and social disorganization, aroused his anxious efforts to interpose the Bible and Christianity as the only effectual antidote. His main hopes rested in the making of Holy Scripture the great organ of mental and spiritual development in education. And this, as usual with him, was a practical opinion. He was all the time working in that field: writing for children, for young men, for Sunday-schools; and his publications of every sort will be found marked with that strong impress of his theory, itself derived from revelation, (for he never was a schemer,) that draughts, pure, direct, and constant, from the fountain of inspired truth, are the most salutary and only sufficient remedy for the evils of the times. To this great result were the incessant productions of his pen addressed, from the series of miniature toy-books for infants, and the Sunday-school "Introduction to the Scriptures," to such profound dissertations as the paper on "Transcendentalism," in the *Repertory*, the joint production of himself and the late Professor Dod, the force and ability of which have made it celebrated as an Evangelical weapon, as well as an exploit in the field of metaphysics. Besides the frequent assistance given, during his professorship, to his brethren in their pulpits, he statedly supplied, for seven years, the colored congregation of Princeton, thus putting himself into contact with a class of persons whose circumstances made his ministry among them a school to himself of the simplicity, so important for every class, but so liable to be forgotten, if not despised, by the scholar.

Who can fail to see in this portion of his life the Providential ordering of circumstances to strengthen and expand his philanthropy, and at the same time to qualify him for his own active exercise of it, on a larger field, and for its more practical inculcation on others? Have the young men of this congregation, and of this city, and I might include in the address the young men every where who have caught the spirit of his writings, reflected that he who threw so much energy and love into their special service, was placed by the hand of Providence—by a dispensation that seemed at the time disastrous—in daily intercourse with scores of young men, far from their homes, as their teacher, as the observer of their minds, dispositions, weaknesses, dangers, their good points and their bad, to raise his qualifications to the maturity of which it was to be your privilege to reap the fruits? And will you not, in the remembrance of these things, after his decease, feel, that, not as a compliment to his memory, not merely as a tribute of your personal gratitude, but out of most solemn recognition of the hand of God in the whole career of your departed friend and Pastor, preceding the bringing of his full and ripe mind to your service—will you not feel that to forget this now, to neglect it because he has gone, to do any thing but strive the more earnestly to hold fast and improve what you have received, will be a mournful, a perilous slight put upon himself, and above all, upon the grace of God, which expended so much to make him what he was to you?

In the Divine purposes, fifty-five years were assigned for the life-time of this his servant. Forty of these had now passed in one steady progress of development to the maturity of character and of capacity, and at least half of that term in active usefulness. Fifteen—only fifteen—remained. Yet even fifteen years is a long space in human life, long enough when it is all industriously consecrated, and under favorable circumstances, to make impressions of which centuries shall not see the end. Luther, though he died at sixty-three, did his predestined work in fifteen years.

And where were the qualifications, whose progress we have been indicating, so likely to find a theatre for their most complete and permanent influence, as in this metropolis? What circumstances could be more favorable for converging the various kinds of talents, acquirements, habits, associations, and experience, which had been combined in the whole preceding career, than those which brought him to the Duane street congregation in 1844—and then, after the necessary interval of rest, furnished by his two years' retirement to the chair in the Theological Seminary at Princeton, (1849–1851,) and an exhilarating voyage to Europe, restored him to his pastoral work here, in 1851? These and subsequent interruptions of his employment as Pastor, let me here say, were submitted to by him as sacrifices, and only in obedience to the duty of preserving his life. When elected to the Seminary, in 1849, he spoke of "the anguish of a separation from my charge, if I accept;" and said: "To *know* that I might remain here, [in Duane street,] would be a joy unspeakable. No dreams of mine respecting the social happiness of the pastoral relation, have failed to be realized." He wrote at the same crisis: "I have seen that my powers were tasked to a tension which must soon be fatal: while in the steadier routine of teaching, I might last a season with ordinary favor of Providence." I quote this to show how peremptory was the necessity of his having relaxation at the time, and how graciously a door was opened, which at once gave him relief, supplied an important station for the benefit of the Church at large, added to his learning, revived his interest in the rising ministry, and prepared him to return to the city, and give the last eight years of his strength and life to the great work reserved for him here.

I deliberately pronounce it a great work, and great not only in the scheme of it, but in its accomplishment. For when we take into consideration what it was to form a new congregation here; to fill this spacious edifice; to gather a band of seven hundred communicants; to form and maintain a successful Mission church; to attract and keep a large body of young men; to not merely win the acceptance, but engage the co-operation of so many, of every age, in his enterprises of doing good; to enlist so much zeal, and to draw out so much liberality; to satisfy such a miscellaneous multitude of hearers; to establish a name and influence outside of his own people, and acknowledged by the community of all classes and denominations—I say, this, that by the favor of God he accomplished, was a great work, in a little time. These walls, this registry of communicants and pew-holders, would not define the limits of your Pastor's zeal, or of his success. His soul suffered at the sight of the destitutions, bodily, social, and spiritual, of the large population of this city, and was always praying to know what he should do for them, and sighing that so little seemed practicable. Willingly would he have thrown open all these seats for the poor. He longed to see the day when churches should be as free as the parks or the streets to all who would come in. Never was he more animated than when originating or assisting some method of reaching the ignorant, degraded, neglected. His philanthropy was more than a lament, a prayer, a whine, a pulpit theory, an anniversary oration, a newspaper rhapsody. He not only talked, but acted, and not only acted, but loved to act; was not only skillful in directing the benevolence of others, but was himself benevolent, and often did the part of benevolence which is far more laborious and self-denying than that which is accomplished by mere giving—though it is not too much to say that his own personal unpublished charities were fully equal, according to the scale of means, to what his influence obtained from others.

In estimating his work in this city, what might I not say of the effect of his personal character, and that, too, as one of the products of Divine grace that qualified him for his position? How could so much of talents and individual influence have been seen connected with so much of simplicity, modesty, and spiritual affections, and not have made a constant impression in favor of his preaching? A minister of the Gospel may be worldly, may be ambitious, may be covetous, may be luxurious, may be indolent. These are the temptations of a large city to ministers as well as to other men. But perhaps the gracious end of your Pastor's afflictions was in no respect more marked than in the influence they had in keeping him, with all the refinement of his tastes, and all his qualifications for literary and social life, so content with domestic retirement and the plodding routine of his parochial work, so conscientious and self-denying as to every thing dangerous or doubtful, so blameless and with such a good report of those who are "without." No American ever visited Europe with more capacity to relish its natural scenery, its historical associations, its seats of learning and repositories of the fine arts, its high refinement and culture; but both his voyages were submitted to as unwelcome but unavoidable separations from his ministry; and in the language of one of his trans-Atlantic letters, (June, 1857,) he could honestly say, "After all, I would a thousandfold rather be at home!" and he meant his ecclesiastical home, his parish, more than his domicile, for his family were with him. No scholar, more than he, enjoyed the employments of literature, but I believe he could always say, as he did when occupying a professor's chair in the College, and at the same time preaching for the blacks once a week: "I believe my happiest hours are spent on Sunday afternoons, in laboring among my little charge."

His personal piety had such prominent features that no observer could do otherwise than take knowledge of its depth and uniformity. What habitual reverence! what engagedness in worship! what hearty intentness in every public exercise! making every one feel that he was acting not with the perfunctory solemnity of a sacred office, but with the personal sincerity of one who felt himself to be a sinner, yet a rejoicing believer and a happy worshipper. How the words of Scripture seemed to take the tone of his own experience! how the pathos of his prayers showed that it was his own soul, as well as yours, he was lifting up to God in confession, praise, and supplication! And who that has heard him, especially in more social assemblies or in the worship at his own fireside, or in the room of sickness and the house of affliction, does not remember how his deep absorption in devotion and the filial, affectionate nearness of his access to the Father of mercies and God of all comfort, caused him to forget what may be called the conventionalities of prayer, and to pour out his soul, indeed with the most abased humility and profound adoration, yet with a directness, familiarity, minuteness, freedom of expression, which was like the interviews of the patriarchs with the Lord God, "face to face as a man speaketh unto his friend," (Ex. 33,) or like those of the apostle who leaned on his Lord's bosom at the holy table.

In fact, this was the secret of the confidence he inspired, the affection he won, namely, the assurance which all felt that he was what he seemed, that he experienced what he declared, that he exemplified what he taught. It was his personal piety, and its abundant fruits that wrought conviction upon every mind that observed him, that his "rejoicing" might be that of the apostle. "The testimony of his conscience that in simplicity and godly sincerity, not with fleshly wisdom, but by the grace of God, he had had his conversation in the world, and more abundantly toward *you*." (2 Cor. 1.) Your luxurious hospitalities did not tempt him; the license, so often pleaded in cities against clerical straitness, was not taken advantage of by him ; his private habits continued in the Fifth Avenue as simple as they were in Charlotte; and when he refused your generous proposal to increase his stipend, it was not (as has been said) because the revenue from his office was wholy sufficient of itself, but because he would do what he could to obviate the popular prejudice on that subject. Should we not acknowledge all this as a gracious endowment that was to enable this follower of Him who came not to be ministered unto, but to minister, to commend "these things" of the Gospel which he preached, to your remembrance after his decease?

It was this sincerity showing itself in such tender and affectionate sensibility that made its way to every heart. How his eye, his tones, his countenance, his quick attention, testified the delicate tenderness of his inmost soul, when any sorrow, or peril, or joy in another touched his sympathy! He made you feel that he was interested for you, and that his expressions were the feeblest index of the amount of his concern. I am persuaded that neither his outward activity, nor any other demonstrations, revealed fully the extent to which his heart glowed with zeal to see more unity among the followers of Christ, more practical fellowship and coöperation among ministers of the Gospel, especially those of the same communion, more earnest, extended, and indefatigable labor to reach the miseries and sins of such a city as New-York. I am sure it is only the simple truth I utter when I say that his spirit groaned in witnessing the extension of crime, wretchedness, and unbelief, and in the anxiety to see the whole force of the entire Church of Christ brought out to personal devotedness, by direct activity and humble work, as well as liberal donations, in the only cause worth living and dying for.

His views were broad, noble, unselfish, and unjealous. His knowledge was universal.* His character, intellectual and spiritual, was remarkably complete and uniform; its symmetry was not broken, ever and anon, by erratic or irregular deviations; his "this one thing I do," was not some favorite atom occupying his mind by itself, but the one great whole of truth and duty according to the proportions in which it stands in revelation. He was, consequently, eminently safe and worthy of reliance; and if I may be excused for resorting to a familiar classical phrase to express it, he was, like the "sapiens" of the Roman satirist, in himself complete, polished and round,† a man for the whole Church and for all the world.

And now, my brethren of this congregation, and of this community, having made this too desultory sketch of the life and the character of this deceased minister, with the main object in view

* His father was remarkable for the extent of his information, but I remember once making an inquiry of him, and receiving for a reply: "Ask James, he knows every thing."

† "In seipso totus, teres atque rotundus,
Externi ne quid valeat per læve morari."
Hor. Sat. ii. 7.

of making more impressive a sense of your own privileges and responsibilities, by showing how he was trained and guided for your service; what great endowments he thus acquired to be expended for your benefit; what a character he by grace attained, to commend to you the religion of which he was a minister; you must perceive how appropriate is the application of the Apostle's sentiment, that now, after the decease of such a Pastor, you should have always in remembrance just what the Apostle meant by what he called, "these things." Five times in this one chapter he uses the same phrase. At every repetition it is employed to denote the grand practical, indispensable fruits of Gospel truth. "If 'these things' be in you and abound, ye shall not be unfruitful in the knowledge of Christ; but he that lacketh 'these things' is blind; if ye do 'these things,' ye shall never fall; I will not be negligent to put you always in remembrance of 'these things;' moreover I will endeavor that ye may be able after my decease to have 'these things' always in remembrance."

They were these things — the great, practical, saving things of Divine revelation—which were most prominent in his preaching; and if his voice could be heard once more, this day, in the clear, earnest, sincere, affectionate tones in which you have been accustomed to hear him speak to you from this spot, it would say: Have *these things* always in remembrance; remember *me* chiefly as the ambassador of Christ to you; let the messages of truth, which I have delivered, be the most prominent in your recollections; think more of Christ than of me; let not the fondness of your personal regard, and the grief for your loss, cause you to forget, that the immutable doctrine I have taught you, survives all *men* — is independent of their ministry. "I preached not myself, but Christ Jesus, the Lord, and myself, your servant, for Jesus' sake." (2 Cor. 4.) "I have not shunned to declare unto you all the counsel of God." (Acts 20.) Yes, my brethren, you know as well as I do, that if he had the direction of this day's services, he would have the connection of his name with them used supremely for the purpose of recalling to and impressing on your remembrance the words of Christ. I call upon you, therefore, this solemn day, to consider by what a long, arduous, painful process the Divine Providence qualified your former Pastor to serve you with such fidelity; how abundantly he instructed you out of the pure oracles of revealed truth; how every class, age, and condition of his charge, found in him all that can ever be found in such frail vessels as the best of ministers are; his labors, so extended and adapted that each finds some special cause to remember what he did for themselves. I summon you, in the name of Him whose servant he was, to remember how weighty is the obligation on you all to respond to this influence. His time was, in your view indeed, lamentably short; but it was long enough to make eternal consequences vibrate on the issue as to each soul—of life unto life, or of death unto death. It was long enough, if time were all, to have converted every one to Christ, to have brought every believer to Christ's standard of what his disciples should be. And I am sure, I do not exaggerate the fullness with which he declared the whole counsel committed to him, when I say that his preaching, his conversation, his catechetical and other instructions of the young, have been sufficient, as to their substance, to accomplish these results, so far as the administration of the means of grace is sufficient. What a reflection is this for each member of the congregation to make, as you meet to-day, as it were at the silent grave of him who was so lately wearing out his very life to do you good! "My deceased Pastor has taught me enough to convert me from the error of my way, and save my soul from death; he has exhibited, by doctrine and by pattern, what I ought to be as a spiritually-minded believer; he has warned me against worldliness and formalism, as the great cankers of piety; he has shown me what it is to live in the grace of our Lord Jesus, the love of God, and the communion of the Holy Ghost; he has both testified and exemplified the obligation of personal zeal for the kingdom of the Redeemer, an untiring, daily concern for the wants and woes of my fellow-men; in all this, he was not a mere philanthropist, not a theorist dreaming new devices for the remedy of social evils, but an accredited representative of Christ and the Gospel, and so speaking the authoritative messages of God himself; and his mission was to *me;* for it he was prepared by Providence through long years of study, of anguish, and the multiform occupations and experiences of his life, so that it is, as to my own opportunity and responsibility, as if all this had been done and endured for myself." Need I follow out these reflections to their legitimate conclusion? It is too obvious to be missed, too solemn in the very statement to need enforcement. I charge you then, whilst you weep this day in the affectionate commemoration of your Pastor, let the great improvement of the event be, to have in remembrance, now after his decease, and always, the things which, in the name of his Lord and Master, he spake while he was yet with you. The highest honor to his memory, the best tribute to his character, the most suitable attestation to his fidelity, will be your steadfast adherence to the doctrines delivered to you. This will show that the distinction of his ministry among you was not that of temporary popularity, nor only of personal attachment, but of his having been received by you for the truth's sake—for Christ's sake.

Some allow themselves to become so attached to a particular minister, that it may almost be said that their religion consists in admiring *him*. Apart from *his* preaching, they scarcely recognize the value of the ordinances of the Lord's house: and when he is removed, they lament as if nothing was left. But the decease of such a minister is a still louder call on those who have heard him, while living, only to be pleased, but not to be regarded. I am heard by some now who are reminded of his faithful but tender expostulations with them in private as well as in public—by notes and letters as well as by pointed sermons: will you not now perceive that God has taken away your human reliance, that he might make you hear more distinctly His own divine voice: removed the human mediator that you might feel that there is in truth but one effectual Mediator, Christ Jesus, and that to Him you must go forthwith and directly? If you have neglected your beloved Pastor, as to the highest purpose for which he was sent to you, beware how you now put from your remembrance, after his decease, the things that belong to your peace, and which, otherwise may, like himself, be soon hidden from your eyes. Listen while I reproduce a few paragraphs from a well-remembered and prophetic discourse which he addressed to a congregation in this city, but a few weeks before he left his pulpit to be seen in it no more: "Ministers of the Gospel often lament in secret over the indifference with which their messages are heard, and sometimes they forecast a time, after their decease, when their words may come back to these hearers with a prevailing force. In this way, as well as others, dead ministers continue to preach. It is wise to cherish their memory. Remember, them . . . which have spoken unto you the word of God; whose faith follow. . . Ah! my respected but unconverted hearers, we come to you, after many trials of preparation and with much consciousness of infirmity, sermon after sermon, Sabbath after Sabbath, month after month, year after year; we grow gray and feeble waiting on you with the Lord's message, which you will not consider; and then we die and you are released from the distasteful reiteration of warning and entreaty.

God grant that the day may not come when you shall gaze on some marble and wish us back; and when echo shall seem to say with Samuel—'Wherefore then dost thou ask of me, seeing the Lord is departed from thee, and is become thine enemy?' Suppose we could return all ghastly to stand beside your death-bed, we could bring you no gospel which you have not rejected. Nothing will have come upon you but that which we had predicted. You have been forewarned; so was Saul. Hence the prophet whom he invokes says to him: 'And the Lord hath done to him as he spake by me . . . because thou obeyedst not the voice of the Lord.'"

This comes to you now as a voice from the grave of your Pastor — the very voice you once heard audibly pronounce these very words, and at the sound of which you trembled, but said, "Go thy way for this time"—when you return once more we *will* give heed!

Turn now, every one who has been under this ministry for years, and only to defer repentance, and then all that we foolishly call the mystery of Providence in causing such a saint to be such a sufferer, and in removing him in the very height of his power, will be explained, sufficiently at least for your satisfaction, in making effectual by the fact of his death what failed to be effectual by the continuance of his life. You would not turn for the living pastor, oh! turn now in the remembrance of his warnings, after his decease!

Cherish, people of his charge, cherish and fulfill his plans. They were the result of long and mature thought, wide observation, long experience, and fervent prayer, and are not likely to be suddenly or easily improved. By thus building on the foundation he has laid, you may continue to enjoy his wisdom and piety in some of their most substantial effects: and happy will it be if the Timotheus who shall succeed this Paul "shall [in this sense] bring you into remembrance of HIS WAYS which be in Christ," (1 Cor. 4,) as well as in the larger sense, call upon you to remember him who has spoken unto you the word of God; whose faith follow, considering the end of his conversation, "Jesus Christ, the same yesterday and to-day, and forever." (Heb. 13.) It will then be as if he were still "abiding and continuing with you all for your furtherance and joy of faith:" and it may be, dear brethren, no extravagant or unscriptural conception to continue the citation, even though we now speak in the name of a minister after his decease—"only let your conversation be as it becometh the Gospel of Christ—that whether I come and see you, or ELSE BE ABSENT, I may HEAR of your affairs, that ye stand fast in one spirit, with one mind striving together for the faith of the Gospel." (Phil. 1.)

Oh! you know that nothing colder than apostolic language would express the heartiness, the warmth, of the interest he felt for your souls! It was with him, as with the writers of the Epistles to the Churches, a labor of love to minister to you. It was without affectation he could address you as "my brethren, dearly beloved and longed for, my joy and crown . . my dearly beloved." (Phil. 4.) "If I be not an apostle unto others, yet doubtless I am to you: for the seal of mine apostleship are ye in the Lord." (1 Cor. 9.) 'We were gentle among you, even as a nurse cherisheth her [own] children; so being affectionately desirous of you, we were willing to have imparted unto you, not the Gospel of God only, but also our own souls, because ye were dear unto us. . . . Ye are witnesses, and God also, how holily and justly and unblamably we behaved ourselves among you that believe: as ye know how we exhorted and comforted and charged every one of you, as a father doth his children, that ye would walk worthy of God, who hath called you unto his kingdom and glory." (1 Thess. 2.)

Yes, my brethren, we speak of the *decease* of our beloved Alexander: but the word has lost its true meaning—that of *departure*—by our customary associations. It is in the original EXODUS, a going out of, the very word used in the narrative of the Transfiguration, when Moses and Elias spoke of the "decease," the exodus, the departure, of the Lord Jesus which he should accomplish at Jerusalem. (Luke 9.) The decease of Christ was his passage to the Father's glory: it was as one continuous event with his Resurrection and Ascension. And so, that departed but everliving Redeemer, says this day as truly as when he spoke similar words in Bethany, of one then in his grave, "Our friend Alexander SLEEPETH; but I go that I may awake him out of sleep." Note how the Son of God identifies himself alike with his living and departed disciples —"*our* friend Lazarus." Then our friend is not dead: he sleeps and does well: for the Resurrection and the Life, in whom he believed, has declared that he "shall never die." Oh! how such a man must enjoy heaven! What a relish and capacity for it was his soul acquiring all his life! What a preparation for this were his years of sorrow and of toil! Yes! he was confident he was approaching all this, when he cried: "I know whom I have believed, and am persuaded that he is able to keep that which I have committed unto him against that day." (2 Tim. 1.) Here we may well stop. May his God and our God so keep us all, that we fail not to follow him and the happy multitudes who through faith and patience inherit the promises!

INSCRIPTION on the Tablet erected by the congregation on the left of the pulpit of the church:

IN MEMORY OF

JAMES WADDEL ALEXANDER, D. D.,

FOR 13 YEARS

THE BELOVED AND REVERED PASTOR

OF THIS CHURCH;

WHOSE SINGULAR NATURAL GIFTS,

RIPENED BY GENEROUS CULTURE,

WERE SUCCESSFULLY GIVEN

TO HIS SACRED WORK:

AND WHO, BY HIS FERVENT PIETY,

PURE LIFE,

TENDER AFFECTIONS, LARGE BENEVOLENCE,

AND UNSPARING LABOUR,

SO ENDEARED HIMSELF TO HIS PEOPLE,

THAT THEY MOURN

AS FOR A DEAR BROTHER AND BELOVED FRIEND.

HE WAS BORN MARCH 13TH, 1804.

HE DIED JULY 31ST, 1859,

DECLARING,

AS THE SUM OF HIS FAITH AND HOPE:

"I know whom I have believed, and am persuaded that he is able to keep that which I have committed to him against that day."

www.ingramcontent.com/pod-product-compliance
Lightning Source LLC
LaVergne TN
LVHW011121110826
845150LV00008B/2208

* 9 7 8 1 4 2 5 5 0 2 9 7 3 *